JULIAN DELPHIKI

UPDATED EDITION

WEB ANALYTICS & BIG DATA

IMPROVE YOUR E-COMMERCE METRICS
ONLINE INSIGHTS TO SELL MORE
EXPLORE THE BIG DATA WORLD

WEB ANALYTICS & BIG DATA

Improve your e-Commerce metrics, online insights to sell more and explore the Big Data world

- Julian Delphiki -

Copyright © 2025 Julian Delphiki

All rights reserved. No part of this publication may be reproduced, distributed, or transmitted in any form or by any means, including photocopying, recording, or other electronic or mechanical methods, without the prior written permission of the publisher, except in the case of brief quotations embodied in critical reviews and certain other noncommercial uses permitted by copyright law.

Web Analytics & Big Data / Julian Delphiki – 1st Edition

ISBN 9798642907672

INDEX

STATE OF WEB ANALYTICS

    FROM THE TRUTH TO INDICATIVE METRICS

    CONSENT MODE

    GA4, THE INEVITABLE

    FROM REAL-TIME DATA TO AI-ENHACED DATA

THE BASICS

    WEB ANALYTICS COMPONENTS

    GOALS, MEASURES AND KPIS

    IMPLEMENTATION

DATA FRAMEWORKS

    REAL-TIME REPORTS

    THE AUDIENCE SECTION

    THE ACQUISITION SECTION

    THE BEHAVIOR SECTION

    THE CONVERSION SECTION

    ECOMMERCE SECTION

SEGMENTATIONS & REPORTS

DASHBOARDS

TEST AND OPTIMIZATION

BIG DATA

    THE ORIGINS OF BIG DATA

USES OF BIG DATA

PRIVACY, SECURITY AND THE FUTURE

CAPTURE, PROCESS, VISUALIZE, ANALYZE, APPLY AND REVERT

CAPTURE

PROCESS

VISUALIZE

GLOSSARY

ABOUT JULIAN DELPHIKI

OTHER BOOKS BY THE AUTHOR

PART I
WEB ANALYTICS

STATE OF BUSINESS ANALYTICS

In this edition, I have introduced a new chapter that delves into the latest trends and developments in web analytics, highlighting their significant impact on businesses. This chapter serves as a comprehensive guide to understanding the current state of web analytics, focusing on key advancements and their practical implications.

Web analytics has evolved dramatically, driven by the rapid growth of data and the increasing sophistication of analytical tools. Businesses now have access to a wealth of information, enabling them to gain deeper insights into customer behavior and make more informed decisions. This chapter explores several main trends shaping the landscape of web analytics today.

The integration of artificial intelligence and machine learning has revolutionized web analytics. These technologies allow for more precise data analysis and predictive modeling, enabling businesses to anticipate customer needs and optimize their strategies accordingly. The ability to process vast amounts of data quickly and accurately has become a game-changer, offering unparalleled opportunities for personalization and targeted marketing.

There is a growing emphasis on real-time analytics. In an era where consumer preferences can shift rapidly, having access to up-to-the-minute data is crucial. Real-time analytics empower businesses to respond swiftly to emerging trends, adjust their campaigns on the fly, and improve the customer experience. This immediacy is particularly valuable in competitive markets where agility can be a decisive factor.

The importance of data privacy and security has come to the forefront. With increasing regulations such as GDPR and CCPA, businesses must navigate the complexities of compliance while maintaining robust analytics practices. This chapter discusses how companies can balance the need for insightful data with the imperative of protecting user privacy, ensuring they remain trustworthy stewards of consumer information.

Another critical trend is the shift towards more sophisticated attribution models. Understanding the customer journey has always been a challenge, but new methodologies are making it easier to track and analyze interactions across multiple touchpoints. Advanced attribution models provide a clearer picture of which marketing efforts are most effective, allowing businesses to allocate resources more efficiently and maximize ROI.

The rise of mobile and omnichannel analytics is transforming how businesses approach customer engagement. With consumers interacting with brands across various devices and platforms, having a cohesive view of these interactions is essential.

Maybe the order is questionable, as probably this new chapter is the most advanced by far. At the same time, I want to honor the freshness of the content and approach these topics first.

FROM THE TRUTH TO INDICATIVE METRICS

With the latest developments in data privacy, the implementation of consent modes, the widespread use of ad blockers, and the inherent limitations of sampling data in GA4, digital marketers face a significant challenge. These changes have introduced a new landscape where data collection is not as comprehensive as it once was. Consequently, web analytics must now be viewed more as a compass guiding us through trends and patterns rather than a complete, detailed picture of user behavior.

Data privacy regulations, such as the GDPR and CCPA, have tightened the rules around how user data can be collected and used. Users are now more informed about their privacy rights and are exercising them, often opting out of tracking and data collection. This increased awareness and regulation mean that a large portion of user data is no longer available for analysis. Consent modes, like Google's Consent Mode v2, aim to navigate these regulations by allowing data collection based on user consent. However, this means that only partial data is available, limited to those users who have explicitly allowed their data to be tracked.

Ad blockers add another layer of complexity to data collection. With the growing use of these tools, a significant segment of web traffic is effectively invisible to traditional analytics tools. Ad blockers prevent the tracking scripts from running, which means that the interactions of these users go unrecorded. This results in a gap in the data, making it harder to get a complete view of user behavior and engagement.

Additionally, Google Analytics 4 (GA4) introduces another layer of complexity through its use of data sampling. Unlike its predecessor, GA4 often relies on sampled data, especially when dealing with large datasets or custom reporting. Sampling can lead to approximations that, while useful, are not always entirely accurate. This introduces another limitation to the precision of the data collected, further emphasizing the need to view web analytics as a directional tool rather than a definitive source of truth.

Given these developments, web analytics can no longer be relied upon for a full, detailed view of what is happening on websites. Instead, it serves as a directional tool, providing insights and trends that can guide marketing strategies. This compass-like role helps marketers understand general user behavior, identify broad trends, and make informed decisions based on the available data. However, it is crucial to recognize that this data is incomplete and should be interpreted with caution.

In this new environment, the key is to adapt and find new ways to understand and engage with audiences. This might involve combining web analytics with other data sources, such as user feedback, surveys, and qualitative research, to fill in the gaps and create a more holistic view of user behavior. Additionally, marketers need to be agile and ready to adjust their strategies based on the insights provided by their compass-like analytics.

The shift towards privacy and the increasing use of ad blockers, along with the implications of data sampling in GA4, are reshaping the landscape of digital marketing. While web analytics remains a valuable tool, its role has evolved. It is no longer the definitive source of truth but a guide that helps marketers navigate the complexities of user behavior in an era of incomplete data. Embracing this new perspective is essential for successfully adapting to the changing digital landscape.

CONSENT MODE

2024 is a pivotal year for digital marketers, largely due to Google Chrome's decision to phase out third-party cookies. This move follows in the footsteps of Safari and Firefox, which made this transition several years ago. However, the impact is far greater with Chrome, as it commands approximately 60% of the global web browser market. Unlike its predecessors, Chrome is not eliminating third-party cookies abruptly. Instead, it introduces new "privacy-friendly" APIs designed to replace the functionality of third-party cookies.

As you're likely aware, third-party cookies have been fundamental for granular remarketing, allowing advertisers to create detailed user profiles and target visitors with tailored ads. However, this practice has raised significant privacy concerns. Google's new APIs aim to establish a more privacy-friendly ecosystem for remarketing and advertising. These APIs function in various ways to achieve this goal, according to Google.

A key aspect of the new approach in Chrome is contextual marketing. This method targets users based on their interests as part of larger groups rather than as individuals. This shift from individual tracking to group-based targeting represents a significant change in how digital marketing operates.

The phasing out of third-party cookies has far-reaching implications for digital marketers and companies that must adapt to these changes. From a Consent Mode v2 perspective, the focus is on helping website owners optimize their ad campaigns and build audiences within the Google ecosystem in this new third-party-cookie-less environment.

So, how does this work? While the process is still evolving and Chrome is gradually removing third-party cookies and implementing the new APIs, some details are emerging. One of these new APIs, the Protected Audience API, integrates with features in Google Ads and GA4. This API can determine if a user falls within a specific "context," such as being interested in cars or other topics. It also facilitates conversions, primarily within Google Ads, but these features are also available in GA4, allowing you to see conversions without switching back to Google Ads.

Complementing these developments is Consent Mode v2, which aligns with Google's privacy-focused ecosystem. Consent Mode v2 sends signals directly to GA4 and Ads, ensuring that data collection is accompanied by instructions based on user consent for statistical or marketing purposes. The two new ad-related flags in Consent Mode v2 guide Google on what the visitor consents to, dictating what Google can do with the data within the third-party-cookie-less Chrome ecosystem and in reporting within GA4 and Ads.

Initially launched in 2020, Google Consent Mode allowed for data collection in compliance with EU data privacy laws (GDPR) for Google Analytics and Google Ads. The updated Google Consent Mode V2 aligns with the Digital Markets Act, effective from March 2024, introducing enhanced features to further support compliance.

However, Google Consent Mode is not a substitute for a Consent Management Platform (CMP) or a cookie consent banner/widget. It does not manage user consent or ensure cookie compliance independently. Instead, it functions as a complementary feature, working alongside a CMP to ensure Google tags and scripts respect users' consent preferences.

Consent Mode v2 is a critical component of Google's new privacy-centric approach. It ensures that website owners can continue to optimize their ad campaigns and build audiences effectively, even as the landscape shifts away from third-party cookies. The interconnected nature of these tools within Chrome, GA4, and Google Ads underscores the integrated strategy Google is employing to navigate this new era of digital marketing.

Google Consent Mode is a tool developed by Google to communicate visitors' cookie consent choices to Google tags. This tool is essential for measuring the performance of your digital channels and advertising while adhering to privacy regulations. By integrating Consent Mode, Google also provides the ability to model the behavior of users who did not grant consent, ensuring comprehensive data insights.

The API of Google Consent Mode utilizes four tag settings to operate:

Analytics_storage: Requests user consent for data usage in analytics.

Ad_storage: Requests user consent for data usage in advertising.

Ad_user_data (new): Requests user consent for using their personal data for advertising.

Ad_personalization (new): Requests user consent for data usage in remarketing.

Based on user interaction with the cookie banner, consent status is either "granted" or "denied." The implementation method chosen—basic or advanced—determines how this information is processed and communicated to Google platforms.

In the basic method, all tags are blocked by firing rules in Google Tag Manager (GTM) and are triggered only when the appropriate consent is granted. This means no information is shared with Google platforms if cookies are not accepted, resulting in no cookieless pings or data modeling from anonymized data.

The advanced method removes triggering rules in GTM, allowing tags to fire and adjust behavior based on the consent level for each tag setting. When consent is not granted, cookieless pings are used to model non-consented visitor behavior and calculate estimated conversions.

If Google Consent Mode is not activated, particularly the updated V2 version, your implementation will lack the functionality needed to process data for the new parameters (ad_user_data and ad_personalization). Without Consent Mode, no data will be sent to your Google advertising platforms. This results in diminished measurement, reporting, audience creation, and remarketing capabilities, leading to less optimized marketing campaigns.

To ensure optimal functionality and compliance, updating to Google Consent Mode V2 is crucial, providing the full range of features necessary for comprehensive data processing and user behavior modeling.

GA4, THE INEVITABLE

In October 2020, Google launched a new version of its web analytics service, Google Analytics 4 (GA4), which has become the default for Google Analytics (GA). This service collects data and analyzes web traffic for millions of businesses, helping them monitor marketing channels and measure Key Performance Indicators (KPIs). GA4 introduces several features that distinguish it from its predecessor, Universal Analytics (UA), with the primary goal of analyzing user behavior and tracking their journey toward becoming customers.

One of the standout features of GA4 is its advanced data modeling capability, which leverages behavior modeling to fill in gaps left by UA. This is particularly valuable as it provides insights into user behavior and website traffic without relying on each page's hits. GA4 also boasts a revamped user interface (UI), distinct from UA, making it more user-friendly and efficient.

GA4 is built on the same platform as the "App + Web" system released by Google in 2019. This foundation allows marketers to track users seamlessly across applications, software, and websites, offering a holistic view of user interactions. This cross-platform tracking is critical as it enables businesses to understand how users transition between different platforms, which has historically been challenging.

The primary purpose of GA4, according to Google, is to offer a next-generation approach to AI-based predictive data, privacy-first tracking, and cross-platform measurement. Its advanced machine learning (ML) models can predict user behavior and provide insights even when traditional data collection methods are limited due to increasing privacy concerns and regulations like the California Consumer Privacy Act (CCPA) and the General Data Protection Regulation (GDPR). This makes GA4 particularly useful in an environment where website visitors are more likely to opt out of cookie usage and other data collection methods.

One of GA4's significant advantages is its seamless integration with Google tools, including YouTube and Google Ads. This integration enhances the ability to track and evaluate YouTube advertising campaigns, measure view-through conversions, and analyze website events. The deeper integration with Google Ads allows for more targeted and effective campaigns, ensuring that offers are relevant and useful to specific audiences, regardless of the device they are using.

Moreover, GA4 offers free access to the BigQuery Export feature, previously available only to paid UA users. This feature allows users to export data to BigQuery cloud storage for more extensive analysis, providing greater flexibility and control over data handling.

The ML and natural language processing (NLP) capabilities of GA4 are among its most significant benefits. These technologies enable users to predict conversion probabilities and create targeted audiences for Google Ads. Users can also receive notifications on conversion trends and predict customer behavior, allowing for more informed marketing strategies and investment decisions. Google plans to continue enhancing GA4's predictive capabilities, including forecasts like average revenue per user (ARPU), which will further aid businesses in optimizing their return on investment (ROI).

One of the critical differences between GA4 and UA is how they handle events and sessions. GA4 uses an event-based approach to analytics, standardizing data collection across multiple platforms, which improves data quality and provides a unified report of visitor paths. This approach contrasts with UA's reliance on visitor sessions, which include various hit types such as events, eCommerce, page, and social interaction hits. In GA4, every interaction is treated as an event, simplifying the data structure and enhancing the accuracy of the insights.

Migrating from UA to GA4 requires understanding these differences, particularly in event handling and session definitions. For instance, UA events have a category, action, and label, while GA4 does not recognize these concepts. Instead, each hit in GA4 is an event, necessitating a new event structure for data collection.

Additionally, GA4 sessions are defined by the session_start event and can end based on the period between events, leading to differences in how active users are counted compared to UA.

GA4's AI and ML capabilities significantly enhance its analytical power, enabling it to predict trends and provide actionable insights. The codeless tracking feature allows users to track events in real-time without coding knowledge, making it accessible to a broader audience. This feature, combined with GA4's ability to track video interactions, offers a comprehensive view of user engagement, including real-time video view counts.

Google Analytics 4 represents a significant evolution in web analytics, offering advanced capabilities for cross-platform tracking, predictive analytics, and privacy-conscious data collection. Its integration with other Google tools and free access to BigQuery Export make it a powerful tool for businesses looking to optimize their marketing strategies and improve their ROI.

As privacy laws continue to evolve, GA4's adaptive features ensure that businesses can continue to gather valuable insights while respecting user privacy.

FROM REAL-TIME DATA TO AI-ENHANCED DATA

AI-powered predictive analytics enables you to identify trends and forecast future outcomes with remarkable precision. This advanced capability is instrumental in making well-informed decisions, impacting everything from product development to marketing campaigns. By leveraging machine learning algorithms, new web analytics solutions offer predictive metrics that help you anticipate user behavior. This foresight allows you to adjust your strategies proactively. Identifying patterns and correlations within vast amounts of data provides actionable insights, ensuring your decisions in areas like product development and marketing campaign planning are data-driven and effective.

Automated user behavior analysis is a significant benefit of AI-driven algorithms, as they can discern patterns and anomalies in real time. This automation eradicates the need for manual data interpretation, delivering immediate, actionable insights. You can quickly understand user interactions and preferences without sifting through extensive datasets. This efficiency translates into better responsiveness and agility in optimizing your strategies.

Predictive analytics, powered by AI, offers the ability to foresee trends and anticipate future user behavior. Whether forecasting website traffic fluctuations or predicting potential conversions, this capability puts you ahead of the curve. With these predictive insights, you can make informed decisions before trends fully materialize, giving you a strategic advantage in planning and execution.

Dynamic personalization is another transformative feature enabled by AI and machine learning. By analyzing individual preferences and engagement histories, tools such as Pathmonk Accelerate can tailor content recommendations to each user. This dynamic personalization enhances the user journey, significantly increasing the likelihood of conversions.

Personalized experiences resonate more with users, fostering engagement and loyalty.

AI-enhanced lead scoring is crucial for identifying high-value prospects efficiently. By assigning predictive lead scores, AI algorithms indicate the likelihood of a visitor becoming a qualified lead. This automated process streamlines the identification of potential customers, allowing you to prioritize and tailor your outreach efforts effectively. With AI-enhanced lead scoring, you can focus your resources on the most promising leads, optimizing your sales and marketing efforts for better results.

In summary, AI-powered predictive analytics revolutionizes how you interpret and act on data. From automating user behavior analysis to providing predictive insights and enabling dynamic personalization, these advanced tools empower you to make informed, strategic decisions. AI-enhanced lead scoring further streamlines your processes, ensuring you target the right prospects with precision. Embracing these AI-driven capabilities not only enhances your decision-making but also positions you to stay ahead in an increasingly competitive landscape.

THE BASICS

Pretty much everything a user does on the web – the sites they visit, the links they click, the videos they watch, and so on – can be stored as data and used to improve understanding of how people are behaving online. That means that if any of those sites, links or videos belong to you, you can access that data to see… well, more or less whatever you want to, whether that is the value of purchases made on your site, the number of people clicking your email link on a mobile device, or the average length of time people spend watching your social video. Most importantly, gathering and interpreting this data allows you to improve your tactics – if you can see what is working (and what is not!), you can learn from it, and use the information to continuously optimize your performance.

In order to do this, you will need an analytics tool. Google Analytics is one of the most internationally well-recognized tools for this, so that is the one we will be focusing on – but the basic principles of collecting and using data apply no matter which tool you are using.

WEB ANALYTICS COMPONENTS

The term web analytics first came about in the late nineties as a way to describe working with the data you collected from your website. More recently, capabilities have expanded to record visitor behavior across your digital presence, including social media, email marketing and paid search – and, where possible, combining these to give you a more complete picture of your customers online.

This wider process is often referred to as 'digital analytics' - so if you ever hear someone using that term, that is what they are referring to. Of course, the concept of measuring, reporting on and optimizing marketing activity existed long before the web we know today came about – so what is special about web analytics?

Web and other forms of digital analytics are unique because of the sheer quantity of information that can be gathered. With television audiences, you know which programs were shown, but you do not know how many people actually watched in each household. You can find the sales figures of newspapers and magazines, but not how many different people may have read each one, or which specific pages they looked at. You might know the number of cars that travelled on a motorway in a given timeframe, but you cannot tell how many passengers in those cars saw the billboards along the way. In the case of the web however, you can find the number of unique users who saw a video, which pages of your site were viewed by how many people, and the number of people who saw your banner ad, clicked it, and went on to make a purchase.

Not only is there much more – and more detailed - data available online - digital technology also allows for that data to be stored, segmented, filtered and analyzed in never before seen ways. And that means you can use analytics data not only to improve your digital activity, but also to conduct market research to understand your customers at a much deeper level; to refine and develop your products and services; and ultimately to improve your entire business strategy. So, how is it done?

We will talk you through all the technical aspects of implementation later on – for now, we will just look at two basic methods used in collecting analytics data. The first way of collecting analytics data is by using server logs. When a user arrives at your site, a request is sent to the web server where your site is hosted to load all of the files that make up your webpage. Each time this happens, the web server makes log entry of what it did. These logs also contain information on the visitor, like their IP address, which can then be used to identify their location or Internet Service Provider.

This information can then be accessed by analytics tools. However, these log files contain a lot of information, so they are often very large and require a lot of processing power – meaning they are not widely used.

The second method uses tracking codes or tags. Google Analytics and many other online tools use JavaScript code which you can place into the areas of your website (or other digital activity) you want to track. When a user takes the action relevant to that tracking tag, the script executes and collects data about where the visitor is coming from, technical information such as the browser and device type, and any cookies that are used by or shared with this tool. Google's Universal Analytics offers three versions of their tracking code, allowing you to look at your web analytics data in conjunction with user data collected from your mobile apps, or any other connected devices.

Tracking codes are relatively easy to implement, and once they are there all the data collection happens automatically within your chosen tool, so they tend to be the preferred method. But what are your tracking codes actually tracking? There are hundreds of aspects of user activity that you might consider measuring, and we will take a look at some of those in detail later in the chapter. Let us focus now on some of the terminology used for different areas of activity you might want your codes to track...

A tracking code might be used to record the number of unique visitors (or unique users) – in other words, the number of different individuals who visit your website. Measuring unique visitors alone does not take into account the number of times each person visited, or how long they stayed for.

A session is the term used to describe one continuous period of time that a user spends on your site. During one session a user might visit several pages, watch a video, download a file, and purchase a product. The session ends when the visitor has not done anything for a specific time, which is usually set at 30 minutes (although this can be changed).

The individual actions taken by a user during the session are known as events. Clicking links, watching videos, and downloading files are all examples of events. It is worth noting that events are not usually recorded automatically by standard page tracking, and you need to add extra code if you want them to be included in your tool's reports. But it is well worth the effort. You can gain very valuable information about which content is engaging visitors and persuading them towards your goals (and which content no-one actually cares about!).

Although there might be plenty of events occurring on your site, there will be one or two major events that you consider as conversions – in other words, the main action you wanted a user to take as a result of visiting and engaging with your site. Examples include making a purchase, filling in an enquiry form or signing up for a newsletter. And by recording the number of unique visitors and the number of conversions, you can identify your conversion rate – the percentage of visitors to your site who end up completing the desired action.

So, you can track how many of your visitors watched a video on your product page, or ended up downloading your brochure.

Where web analytics really stands out though is the ability to drill down even further into this data. This is where dimensions come in. Say you wanted to see all the different countries your visitors were coming from, or all the devices being used to access your site – these would be classed as dimensions. They form the rows in your analytics reports. You can add secondary dimensions too – so under each country you could add dimensions showing you the devices being used there.

Metrics, on the other hand, form the columns in your report. They are always numeric measurements (including percentages or ratios). They show you how many times a particular action was taken by each dimension you have set – so conversion rate is a metric that could show you how many visitors in each country bought a certain product.

Before we go any further, it is important to understand that your analytics data, while useful, cannot be seen as scientifically accurate.

There are a few reasons why this is the case. First up, if you are using the free version of Google Analytics and you have high traffic volumes, your data might be sampled to save processing resources. This means that only a subset of your visitors is reported on, and so the results might not be typical of other visitors whose behavior was not included in the report. If sampling is being used for the current report, there will be a message at the top of the screen to let you know. Then there is the issue of standards. Although most analytics tools will offer a similar set of things you can measure, there are no universally accepted standards about certain aspects of measurement – how long a user needs to watch a video before it counts as a 'view,' for example. That means you cannot really compare analytics data provided by one reporting tool with information from another.

Tracking users also presents some technical issues that put limitations on the accuracy of your data. Any data collected by analytics tools has to be anonymous – you are not allowed to store any personally identifiable information (or PII) on your visitors, including email addresses or telephone numbers. That means the data you use to identify audience demographics on your site has to be obtained through cookies supplied by advertising companies like DoubleClick – and if cookies are not available for every visitor, this data will not represent the complete makeup of your traffic.

Using cookies to track repeat visits also leaves you open to problems of cookie deletion, or 'do not track' requests – not to mention the issues in trying to identify one user who is interacting with your digital presence across several different devices or browsers.

So, analytics data cannot give you 'auditable' numbers. But it is still incredibly useful to show you how your digital activity is performing across all channels so you can optimize and improve your strategy on an ongoing basis.

GOALS, MEASURES AND KPIS

When you think about all the different metrics you could measure for what is happening on your site, and all the different categories of information about your visitors, you start to realize just how many options there are when it comes to analytics! But, if you start trying to measure and report on everything you can think of, you are going to be overwhelmed by data pretty quickly - and it is going to be hard to focus on a specific area for improvement. You need to narrow it down so that you are only reporting on what is really important for your business – and that starts with identifying your goals and objectives. An objective is an overall statement of why your company is in business in the first place. Obviously, for most companies the primary objective is to make money. For many organizations there may also be secondary objectives – perhaps around increasing awareness of a product or service, or growing geographic reach. Goals describe the steps needed to reach your objectives.

Whichever way you think about this, the point of goals is to help you reach your business objectives by making it clear what you are trying to achieve, and how you will know when you have achieved it. So, your goals should be clearly linked to your objectives, and they should be designed to help you evaluate progress in a realistic, practical way that makes sense.

A quick word of warning: Google Analytics uses the term 'goals' to mean conversions or desired outcomes of a visit. These analytics goals are not the same as your business goals, so make sure you distinguish between the two when you are discussing them! When you are defining analytics goals, you might be tempted to focus on the ones that most obviously make you money, such as sales or lead generation.

Goals that relate to your primary business objectives like these are referred to as macro goals. Macro goals can be useful – but relatively few users coming to your site are actually going to undertake these on first visit. That is why you will also need to identify your micro goals – the ones that do not earn you immediate revenue, but help to build towards that by keeping users engaged or persuading them to come back again later. Regardless of whether they are macro or micro goals, it is helpful to assign a value to them so that you can evaluate how well your site and marketing are working. It is easy enough to see how this might work for goals that relate closely to revenue, and therefore have a monetary value attached to them anyway. What is more difficult is to identify the value of non-revenue generating micro goals – how do you estimate the value of a video watched, or a sign-up to your email newsletter? You might approach this scientifically. By talking to other people in your organization – your sales team, for example – you might be able to estimate the revenue they would expect to get following completion of your micro goals.

Do not worry if that is not possible though – it is also valid to use a non-revenue related number as a relative goal value. For example: if visitors download a product brochure, they are presumably at least interested in knowing more, and might make a purchase in the future. You could assign this goal a notional value of "2". If visitors check out your shipping costs, they may be seriously considering a purchase – so you could assign that a relative value of "5". Having numeric values in your reports really helps compare different conversions and evaluate the relative impact of any changes you have made. So, if at all possible, do not leave the goal value blank – if you are not sure, it is better to just assign a simple notional value of '1'.

Your goals and objectives define what you want to achieve – but how do you check whether you are on the right track? For that you will need KPIs. KPI stands for Key Performance Indicator. KPIs are essentially your most important metrics – the ones that show you how well you are doing against your business goals.

They need to be focused and well-defined – so if you find you are coming out with more than six or seven, it is likely that you have not set your priorities quite clearly enough. The more you have, the harder it becomes to focus your activity on solving the business-critical problems. If you are struggling to narrow down your list, try asking yourself 'what are we going to do when we find out this KPI?' If the answer is 'I do not know,' it is probably not one you need to be too concerned about. Because they are so closely related to your goals, each business will need their own, unique set of KPIs. For example, Average Order Value might be a KPI for an eCommerce site, whereas a newspaper site which depends on advertising revenue would be much more focused on the number of pageviews and repeat visitors.

When creating your list of KPIs, it can be helpful to divide them into three categories, which are mirrored in the Google Analytics reporting structure. Ideally, you should define a maximum of two or three KPIs in each area. The three categories are:

• Acquisition KPIs. These measure how you are doing in attracting visitors to your website. Good KPIs in this area will help you to evaluate the return on investment of your marketing budget. Acquisition KPIs are things like Cost per Acquisition (or how much it costs to get a visitor), share of search (or the amount of visibility your keywords achieve in search results) and click-through rate (the percentage of visitors who clicked through to your site from an external link).

- Behavior KPIs. These relate to the actions that visitors take on your site outside of purchases and conversions. Good KPIs in this area will help you evaluate visitors' level of engagement with your content. They include page depth (or the average number of pages viewed per visit), visitor loyalty (or the number of people who came back to your site and how often they did so) and bounce rate. A common misconception is that bounce rate refers to the number of visitors who leave your site 'immediately,' but technically it is calculated as the number of people who leave your site without making a second click – so, even if they leave after spending ten minutes on the landing page, it is still a 'bounce.'

- Conversion KPIs. These metrics relate to business outcomes. Good KPIs in this area will help you evaluate how compelling your calls to action are and the usability of your site. They might include conversion rate (or the percentage of visitors who complete each goal), total goal value (the value you set for that goal, multiplied by the number of times that goal was attained) and average order value.

A common misunderstanding is to think of concepts like "brand awareness" or "customer satisfaction" as KPIs. Of course, you need to know about them, but they are not KPIs, they are actually goals – aspects of your business that you want to improve. To measure them, you will need to produce some associated KPIs - "share of search" is a good example. Say you decide that a KPI for your business is pageviews, or the total number of hits a page receives. You have set up all the right tracking codes, and your analytics tool is telling you that your pageview count is up 50% from last month. Sounds good – but if last month you got two-page views, and this month you got three, you are still not doing very well! Unless you define a target for each KPI, you will have no idea whether the figure in your reports represents success.

When you are setting targets, the same rules apply as they do with setting goals – they should be meaningful and achievable, but they should still represent real progress. You might decide your goal is for pageviews to increase by 100%. In that case, you have identified an area you need to improve – but unless you know what to do about it, the numbers by themselves are meaningless.

That is why you will often need to pick KPIs that drill a little deeper, so you can get actual, actionable insights from them. Instead of pageviews, you might choose to look at page depth – the average number of pages viewed per visit. That way you will still see how many views you are getting, but you will also see whether your content is engaging people – and if it is not, you have identified something concrete on which you can actually work.

Arriving at clear and effective business objectives, goals, KPIs and targets can be tricky – but it is also vital to success. If you feel that the goals that have been set are unclear or unreasonable, it is worth taking the time to rethink them – ignoring problems at this stage will only cause you more difficulties later on.

IMPLEMENTATION

By now you should have a clear idea of what you want to see included in your analytics reports – but you still need to set up and implement your analytics correctly to make sure you are getting the right data! As a rule of thumb, always check your initial reports for any obvious anomalies.

If you have forgotten to implement the tracking code on one of your pages, or if it is generated more than once on the same page, try to catch it as soon as possible! Warning signs of this include a suspiciously low bounce rate, caused by the code loading twice (and therefore making it appear as though there has been a second click) or your own site appearing as a referrer, which suggests the tracking code is missing from the page doing the 'referring.'

Using Google Tag Manager reduces the risk of these things happening, but it is still worth checking your early reports to be sure. When in doubt, follow your instincts – if something does not look right, it probably is not, and it is better to be sure than make business critical decisions using data that might be a bit dodgy.

It is also important to customize your analytics tool so that what it is showing you aligns as closely as possible with what you need. Getting this right at an early stage can significantly impact the effectiveness of your reporting. Within Google Analytics, there are plenty of potential areas for customization.

Filters, for example, are divisions that you apply permanently to your data. They are used to ensure that your reports never contain information which you define as distracting or irrelevant. For example, many companies like to ignore data about activity by their own employees, so that they can concentrate on analyzing visits from existing and potential customers. This can be done by creating a filter to exclude sessions originating from the company's IP address.

In tools like Google Analytics, data that is excluded by a filter is not collected and therefore cannot be recovered at a later date. This means that if your filter is not set up correctly, you will not be able to get back any data you have lost. That is why it is advisable to always keep an unfiltered "Master" profile in your analytics set-up even if you do not use it very often – so you will always have the full set of data available, should you need it.

If you have decided to set up event tracking, you will also need to choose the field values that you want to record for each event. You will start with the event category, which lets you group certain types of element together – for example, video, PDF, or button. Then there is the event action, which is the specific action taken by the user. If your category is video, your actions might be play, pause, view (in which case you will need to decide how long a user has to watch before it counts as a view), and so on. Lastly, there's event label, which lets you name individual items within the same category – so for example, 'intro video,' 'June promotional video,' 'July promotional video.' As you can see, these parameters will potentially give you very detailed information about each event. However, this is only useful if you have thought through exactly what you want to know, and if you are using fields and labels consistently.

Beyond tracking codes, you might also want to think about using extra parameters in the destination URL of your ads or other activity to identify exactly how a user got to your site. For example, you might be running a campaign for the same promotion that includes QR codes in print magazines, and Facebook ads. If you do not add parameters to the URLs for these links, the mobile visitors using the QR codes are likely to show up in your analytics as direct visitors. The Facebook visitors will be listed within all of the referrals from Facebook, but you will not be able to distinguish between the visitors clicking on this specific ad and those clicking on other Facebook posts you have made.

By adding parameters to your landing page links with the same campaign name but specifying the different platforms used, you can identify all of the visitors from this campaign, regardless of where they came from. Then you can isolate these visitors, and evaluate which marketing tactics generated the best return on investment for the campaign overall. As you can imagine, the number of these extra parameters that you are trying to control could become very unwieldy very quickly, so it is well worth using an automated system that can help you quickly add parameters to new campaigns and links, and to reduce the number of errors. Just as with filters, URL parameters cannot be corrected or reworked once they are in place. So, it is important to plan this carefully from the start of any campaign. It is also important to be very consistent when defining and using parameters. Many analytics tools will treat "Facebook" and "Facebook.com" as different items even though they are not. An automated management system can be helpful in ensuring consistency.

Once you have gotten your analytics set up, you will start to see all that data come pouring in. Then you will be able to start looking at what is going on around your online presence, and making those all-important improvements to your activity.

DATA FRAMEWORKS

By now you should know how to collect user data from your site, but the thought of actually opening up your analytics tool and figuring out where all that data lives might still seem a little daunting. We are going to take a look at the different reporting areas within analytics tools, and show you which sections your users' data can be found in and – more importantly – which questions each area can help you to answer.

REAL-TIME REPORTS

These pages in your analytics tool show you live information about visitors who are currently on your site - for example, which pages they are on, where they came from, and some demographic information. This is in contrast to most other analytics reports, where the data updates on a 6 - 24-hour basis. Live reporting allows you to continuously monitor and optimize campaigns and promotions, and to take advantage of current trends and opportunities, like visitors responding to news stories, product reviews, sporting events or celebrity endorsements.

The ability to see real-time activity on your site and the potential for fast response can be very seductive. However, before you leap into action, there are a couple of things to watch out for:

- Do you have enough visitors showing similar behavior to make your conclusions valid? Be careful about acting on the evidence of a small sample alone, since that might not be representative of your whole audience.

- Are you really familiar with your business goals and KPIs, and what your campaigns are trying to achieve? Fast decisions can lead to great results, but they are also dangerous if taken too quickly, or with insufficient understanding of the implications. Say you started running a new social media campaign, but noticed it was not performing well. You might be tempted to cancel it - but it could be that the audience for your new campaign is mostly active at weekends, and you just have not waited long enough to see that yet!

THE AUDIENCE SECTION

This is where you will find information about the characteristics of your visitors, including whether they are new to your site, their geographic locations, their ages and interests, the language that they speak, and technical information about the devices and browsers that they are using to access your site.

Within the audience section, you can find answers to your questions about geographic location: What proportion of your traffic comes from the area your business actually operates in? Are those visitors converting at a reasonable rate? Do you receive significant traffic from any other locations that might suggest you need to make a change to your overall business model?

These reports can also help you understand the makeup of your visitors from the perspective of age, gender, hobbies and purchasing patterns – in other words, their demographics, and interests. For example, you can see whether your traffic skews male or female, younger or older, or what types of products they typically buy. You can then use these insights to refine your content, brand messaging, and advertising copy, making sure that you have the needs of your specific audience in mind.

And then there's mobile devices. Your audience section will tell you what proportion of your traffic accesses your site using a smartphone or tablet compared to desktop usage. How are your mobile conversion rates? Are visitors on mobile devices actually likely to complete a purchase? That is not to say that you should not work on your mobile digital presence, but your analytics data might help you to assign some priorities when allocating budgets and resources.

THE ACQUISITION SECTION

Having looked at the different platforms, let us explore the key points, and potential trade-offs, your social media strategy might face.

You will need to find the balance between declaring and sharing. Remember, content that is exclusively attached to a brand, or feels heavily branded, is rarely the most popular. This could be a difficult trade-off if you are looking at spending a limited budget on your marketing communications overall, and senior managers who aren't social media users themselves may legitimately ask "why do it?"

Then, there is the balancing of targeting and attracting. Social media platforms are tools for digital marketing, and provide a variety of ways to identify and target users, often funneling them to other sites and potential data capture.

Some of the most interesting business uses of social media throw these principles to the wind, however, in the hope of attracting new views from people that may not have emerged from any targeting activity. For example, The Financial Times newspaper chose to publish intriguing charts on Instagram without referrals back to its site; it simply wanted to attract users. With its account now being followed by 1.4 million users, we can safely say it succeeded.

In order to really get the most from your social media presence, there are some key considerations you will need to take into account - starting with your brand voice.

Let us be honest, most companies talk in a voice that is oddly impersonal, if not quite sterile. There is a tendency to use the corporate or royal "we" to announce things, and stuff marketing brochures with descriptive sentences. Press releases are often populated with buzzwords and big claims, but this would most likely fail if the same approach were used on social platforms.

The third reporting area We are going to look at is the Acquisition section. This holds all the information about how your visitors get to your site. All of the various marketing channels that you might use, like organic search, email, social media, and mobile marketing are shown in a report that measures the relative performance of each one. In order to make the most of this section, there are two acquisition terms you need to be familiar with.

Direct traffic refers to visitors who came "directly" to your site, without clicking on a link or going through a search engine. This implies that they already knew the URL of your site or had it bookmarked, so it is generally assumed that they are familiar with your business. For this reason, direct visitors can be an important factor in considering brand awareness.

Referrals, on the other hand, are visitors who arrived at your site by clicking on a link from another website. The referral path in the analytics report shows where they came from. Your acquisition reports will help you understand your advertising return on investment. Obviously, if you are spending money on advertising, it is important to know which campaigns and media are effective in generating conversions. If you have configured your analytics goals correctly, you should be able to review both macro and micro conversions that are associated with paid visits. You can also use these reports to look at goal completions and engagement rates for all channels, helping you to identify which ones are over- or underperforming. Where do your most valuable visits come from? Are there any channels that seem to be either much more, or much less successful than the others? If so, do you have any clues as to why that might be? And how should you readjust your spending and priorities as a result?

The acquisition area will also show you the search queries used in search engines where your site was listed in the results. Since Google usually shows the corporate site in response to searches for a company name, it is usual to see the name of your business in the search query listings. Queries that include a company name are referred to as "branded searches." By definition, visitors searching for your business name have already heard of you. But there are probably many more potential customers who are not familiar with your company. A good search engine optimization strategy should also include "nonbranded" keywords focused on your products and services to attract this wider audience. By reviewing your search queries report, you will be able to evaluate the current strengths and weaknesses of your organic search positions for both branded and nonbranded searches.

And finally, there's social media. If you include social media as part of your marketing mix, it is important to know which platforms produce the best results for you. Again, look at the conversions and other goal completions, as well as engagement metrics such as time spent on key pages. This information should help you to tailor your social media campaigns towards your most valuable audiences.

THE BEHAVIOR SECTION

The Behavior section tells you about what visitors do once they are actually on your site, with a focus on activities other than purchases - these are covered in the Conversions section, which we will talk about in a moment.

Reports in the Behavior section include the specific pages visited, how the site performed in terms of loading speed, details regarding usage of your onsite search engine, and information about any events that you are tracking. You might start off in this area by looking at visitor loyalty. The 'frequency and recency' reports tell you how many times visitors came to your site in a given timeframe. These measures of loyalty can tell you a lot about the effectiveness of your branding campaigns, whether your content is engaging, and how compelling your incentives for repeat business might be.

When viewing these reports, you need to identify a reasonable expectation around returning visitors for your specific business. For example, a news site might want visitors to come every day, whereas an online grocery might expect visitors to place orders once a week.

Content usage reports tell you how specific pages on your site are actually being used. That helps you identify consistently popular content and ensure that you are taking full advantage of these pageviews. You can also tell which pages are rarely being seen. If you have pages that do not draw visitors, you might consider whether that content is simply not interesting to your audience, or whether your site could do better in drawing them to that area. You can also identify 'entry' and 'exit' points – the pages where users arrive and leave your website. If you have a high bounce rate, looking at the content on your entry page might help you work out why. Similarly, if the content on your exit pages is a logical exit point – a thank you page after a transaction, for example – there is nothing to worry about. But if visitors are consistently leaving in the middle of the shopping process, there is probably an issue you need to fix.

THE CONVERSION SECTION

This is where you will find information about how well your site is driving transactions, leads, and any other interactions (macro and micro goals, and events) that you have defined. Most companies tend to focus on this section, because it has the most obvious impact on the business bottom line. However, the key role that Acquisition and Behavior play in generating conversions means you should really pay equal attention to those sections too.

In this section, you might want to check out goal or event completions. This shows which visitors complete your goals and events, which content and pages best motivate them to do so, and in what order. Look for goals and events that are rarely fulfilled as well, especially if they are important to your business. Are there clear obstacles or other reasons that might prevent visitors from completing their tasks?

The conversions section is also where you will go to see your funnel analysis. In order to convert on your site, visitors will have to take a number of specific steps along the way. For example, in the case of a purchase, the customer will need to place an item in the shopping cart, enter their delivery and billing information, confirm the order, and pay. In general, far more visitors will start the process than will finish it, and the funnel allows you to see where they drop out. In theory, if you can locate and identify the issues that cause them to leave, you should be able to improve conversion rates and therefore increase revenue.

Bear in mind that you do not always know the visitor's motivation for doing something, though. They might have added an item to their cart just to research shipping costs, without an immediate intention to purchase. Visitors may enter your funnel at an unexpected point, or skip a step somewhere. The funnel can be a great indicator of patterns in visitor behavior, but do not interpret funnel analysis too literally!

The final part of the Conversions section We are going to talk about is multi-channel attribution. Understandably, marketers need to be able to evaluate which channels and tactics are generating the highest conversion rates, and assign budget accordingly. However, it is pretty unusual that a visitor to your site will convert on their first visit. In fact, it may take several sessions before a user converts, and it is likely that each time they visit your site they will come from different channels.

Multi-channel attribution reports offer the ability to display all of the channels that the visitor used leading up to the transaction, and to assign different values to each one so that you can evaluate the impact of each channel on the end result. Each business will need to work out the attribution model that best suits them, and your analytics tool should be customizable to represent the model of your choice.

Multi-Channel Attribution Marketers should consider how best to use multi-channel reports, usually found in the Conversions section of an analytics tool, to ensure ad spend is effectively distributed. An In Focus Look at Multi-Channel Attribution: To create and maintain an effective digital marketing strategy, marketers need to be able to evaluate which channels and assets are generating the highest conversion rates, and assign budget accordingly.

However, it is pretty unusual that a visitor to your site will convert on their first visit. In fact, it may take several sessions before a user converts, and it is likely that each time they visit your site they will come from different channels. Without a way of definitively understanding and analyzing which channels are providing value along the entire path to conversion, marketers may be prevented from accurately evaluating the value of each channel – often misattributing value to the channel(s) used directly before a conversion. As a result, the channels that are key in driving, for example, consideration may end up being under-funded, making the campaign altogether less effective. This is where multi-channel attribution comes in!

Multi-channel attribution reports offer the ability to display all of the channels that visitors are using along the path to conversion and, importantly, assign different values to each one so that you can accurately evaluate the impact of each channel on the end result and allocate spend appropriately. For example, take UK-based insurance comparison site Confused.com. Confused.com suspected that its ad spend was not accurately representing the value of the channels used in the lead-up to conversion. Using Google Analytics' Attribution tool, it discovered that display advertising was offering value within the consumer journey that was not being accurately reported. Based on these insights, Confused.com increased spending in digital display ads by 500% in the first year whilst still achieving their return on investment goals. So, for a more accurate depiction of the overall value of the channels used in a digital marketing strategy, brands should consider utilizing multi-channel attribution.

ECOMMERCE SECTION

Last but not least, we come to the eCommerce section. As you might have guessed, this is only applicable to sites that actually sell products directly. This section of your reports will help you answer questions on product performance. What are your best-selling products? Are there any surprises here that you could take advantage of with new or further promotions? If you have physical stores too, are there any differences between the top sellers online and offline?

You can also use these reports to look at shopping behavior. Do visitors look at a lot of products, but add very few of them to their shopping carts? Perhaps you need to improve your product descriptions, or add some reviews.

And finally, you might want to look at checkout behavior. How many people abandon their shopping cart, and when in the process is this most likely to happen? For example, do visitors exit after seeing shipping charges or other additional fees?

As you can see, there is quite a lot you could be measuring – and we have only just scratched the surface! Rather than trying to look at it all at once, make sure you identify the areas that correspond to your goals, and use this information as a guide so that you know where to look when it is time to fire up your tool of choice.

SEGMENTATIONS & REPORTS

Now we know how to identify what data is useful to you, how to collect it and where to view it, we need to think about ways to drill even deeper into that data, and come out with some really meaningful insights. And where better to start than with segmentation.

Visitors come to your website for many different reasons, from many different places, and with many different expectations. If you understand this, then it should be clear that you cannot just look at all of your data as though it comes from one homogenous audience.

The segments function of your analytics tool allows you to choose specific criteria that divide your visitors into smaller, more contextualized groups. For example, returning customers are generally more likely to make a purchase on your site than first time visitors. They are already familiar with your products, and they need less background information and reassurance about your returns policies. On the other hand, they are more likely to be interested in your loyalty club. For this reason, it is helpful when reviewing conversion rates and onsite behavior to look at these two groups separately.

A good analytics tool will provide some commonly used "default" segments which are already set up for you, as well as allowing you to create your own custom segments. Google Analytics' defaults can be used to segment your visitors according to the Audience, Acquisition, Behavior and Conversion categories - and they also offer a 'gallery' of free to use segments that other users have found helpful.

Default segments are great to get you started, but with a clear understanding of your business goals and KPIs, you will want to develop your own custom segments.

Let us say your site has a high overall bounce rate. You are also aware that some of your visitors seem to be from a country where your products are not available. By creating a custom segment to exclude these 'unqualified' buyers, you may well find that your bounce rate improves immediately! As always, do not forget it is not just about user activity on your site. If you are using tags to track your advertising campaigns, you can divide your audience into custom segments here too.

Say you want to look at whether a specific campaign worked better in certain cities. You could do this by segmenting by city, and comparing the responses of visitors who saw the campaign with those who did not.

So, you have had a look at your data within your analytics tool, and implemented some useful segments that help you identify patterns in what is going on.

The next step is to create a report. When it comes to producing analytics reports, it is easy enough to just fill page after page with numbers, graphs and charts that look complicated and impressive. The real skill in web analytics is in understanding what those numbers tell you, and using the evidence you have gathered to provide commentary on the current situation, insights, and recommendations for next steps.

Remember that an executive summary of the data itself is not analysis! All of your reporting should focus on the objectives, goals and KPIs of your business, and the potential effects of your findings on your overall bottom line and customer satisfaction. You may well be called on to write long reports with lots of analysis, but if you are presenting to time-poor decision-makers you'll need to answer the following questions clearly and concisely: What have you learned? What do you want us to do, and why? What benefit might we gain from taking action on this? What might be the cost of not doing something about this?

Suggesting business-critical changes can sometimes be nerve-racking because you will never be able to determine the exact outcome before you start – but if you do not act on what your analytics data is telling you, there was really no point in spending all that time collecting and analyzing it.

There is no need to rely on 'gut instinct' though. At the bare minimum, your analytics data should help you demonstrate the current losses or damage being caused by the scenario that you are flagging – but there are options for providing evidence-backed propositions for change. One option is to make estimates using external data. For example, if the industry average cost per click for one of your keywords is less than you are paying, you can estimate the potential savings to be gained by improving your Quality Score.

Case studies about changes and optimization tactics by other businesses can also be a great way to generate support for your recommendations. Once you have explained your recommendations, you will also need to prioritize them according to levels of urgency and importance. Every organization will have its own

process for assigning priorities and deciding the order of implementing recommended changes. However, your report should provide some background and data to help inform management decisions. You will need to answer questions like: How mission-critical is this issue? If you have found an urgent problem for your business - a broken checkout process, for example - then obviously a speedy response is needed. If you have found some typos on a product page, although it may look unprofessional, this might be something that can wait.

How much time, money and resource will this cost? Your management will need to know what it will take to address the issue. As we mentioned before, even if you cannot calculate the exact costs, you need to provide some framework for a budgetary discussion.

What all this comes down to is that a good report – whether it is an executive summary or a deep-dive analysis – needs to be all about identifying issues and proposing solutions, using analytics data as evidence. A good analyst is great with numbers – but they also need to be a great communicator for the whole business to benefit from their skills.

———— ○ · ● · ○ ————

DASHBOARDS

One way you might choose to present your analytics findings is using a dashboard. Dashboards are normally one page (or screen) of information, showing you what is happening in critical areas, how well your most important KPIs are doing, and how your results are trending over time – so you can find everything you need in one place.

It is good practice to create a number of different dashboards, tailoring each one to a specific audience within your business. This is helpful because each manager (or department) can choose to see only the information that is relevant to them. For example, your Chief Financial Officer might want to see revenue and related spending figures, while your Vice President of Sales might be more interested in monitoring improvements to your conversion rates.

So, how do you create one? Your analytics tool might include a default dashboard presentation – the homepage of your Google Analytics account is a good example. This is a useful start, but to make sure that you get optimal insights for your business, it is best to design and customize your own set of dashboards. Your analytics tool should allow for this, and you can also export data to one of the many commercial software programs available.

The key to an effective dashboard is to identify the most critical information to present. As with all methods of reporting, make sure you are offering insights and recommendations with supporting evidence. That means that you need to provide context for the data you are highlighting. Never show a single metric by itself without something to compare it with, or further detail derived from drilling into secondary dimensions or segments.

Julian Delphiki

One of the most important aspects of an effective dashboard are the visuals. Clear, simple but compelling visuals are key to any good analytics report, especially on a dashboard, where you are trying to assemble all the crucial information in one easy to read place. Make sure you choose the type of chart that illustrates your data correctly, whether that is a funnel showing sequential stages, a pie chart or a bar graph.

Whichever chart you choose, it needs to clarify and simplify the information, not make it more complicated. A good visual should be self-explanatory. If the visual itself requires a lot of commentary in order to be understood (as opposed to commentary providing insights and recommendations), then it is not useful. All good visuals have certain elements in common.

Chart titles need to be simple and compelling, and the labels for each axis or area of a graph need to clearly describe what is being shown. Using color well is important too – too many colors can be overwhelming and confusing, but using contrasting colors appropriately can really bring clarity to an image. If you can, try to give something of a narrative to your dashboard and the accompanying commentary.

Many people, especially those who are not data-driven, understand and retain the message of a story much better than they do numbers and graphs. A well told story helps your audience see themselves playing a part in carrying out your recommendations, and increases their engagement and motivation.

And finally, do not forget that the components of your dashboards are not set in stone. Critical metrics for your business will change over time, so do not be afraid to let your dashboard evolve by replacing areas that are no longer important to track with more relevant ones.

Hopefully now you understand how to turn all those data points into something that is easy to read, digest, and action. The most important point to remember is that reports offer evidence-backed insights, not just data out of context – and if you can provide that, you will start seeing improvements to your activity in no time.

Web Analytics and big data

TEST & OPTIMIZATION

We have already shown you that the whole point of analytics is to identify areas where you can optimize performance. But, as you might have expected, it is a bad idea to rush in headfirst and change everything without doing some proper testing first.

Your data will give you a solid indication of where things are going wrong, and should help guide you towards potential solutions. But you will never know if the changes you are making are working unless you try your ideas on actual visitors. On the plus side, there is so much data collected in web analytics – far more than print or broadcast media – those developing theories and then testing the results is relatively easy and inexpensive. And unlike information gained from focus groups and surveys, the analytics data that you gather from testing reflects how visitors respond to your website of their own accord, without prompting or guidance from you. This might sound straightforward, but actually many businesses still are not running this kind of testing at optimal levels due to a lack of employee knowledge and resources.

Any team involved with analytics testing and optimization needs to be confident in creating the initial definition of what should be tested, setting up the right variables, and interpreting the results.

Let us start with deciding what to test. Before you can start investigating anything, you need to create a hypothesis. This is essentially a statement of the theory behind the test, which will be proved or disproved when you come to evaluate your results. Creating hypotheses ensures that you have a clear strategy and are not just testing elements at random or working on the basis of other people's 'best guess' as to what should be done, which can be expensive and unproductive. One word of warning at this point: it is important not to become too attached to your original hypothesis, regardless of whether it turns out to be correct – it is not about 'proving your idea right'! It is not uncommon for even the most experienced practitioners to be surprised by test outcomes.

The value of testing is in what you learn, and any experiment which results in actionable insights is worth running. All good hypotheses should be based on some starting evidence. It is rarely helpful to randomly try changing the placement of a link, or the color of a button without some reason for doing so. That being said, you do not have to wait until your dashboard figures are in meltdown before you start running tests. There is always something you could improve upon, so if there are not any sirens and flashing red lights going off, what could you use to identify helpful areas for experimentation?

First up, of course, is your analytics data. Try looking at the comparison views rather than the standard data charts, to see whether there are any areas which significantly beat or lag behind the site averages. For example, do you have landing pages with unusually high bounce rates, or micro goals with far lower completion rates than you would expect? You might also want to take a look at your visitor feedback. Listening to what visitors tell you about their experience on your site can give you valuable ideas for improvement. You could implement a brief survey on the site, or ask your sales or customer service teams for any frequently voiced complaints. And finally, there's good old-fashioned gut instinct. We have talked so much about data driven decision making that this one might come as a bit of a surprise, but it is perfectly valid to look at elements of your site and recognize areas where you think there might be usability problems. It is usually then worth looking into the analytics data to see if your suspicions are backed up by the numbers, and to gather a little more evidence. For example, you might suspect that a lead generation form has too many fields, and your analytics might show that a similar form with fewer fields has a higher conversion rate. There may ultimately prove to be no relationship between the two, but at least you now have a starting point for investigation!

Once you have identified what you want to test, it is good practice to construct a hypothesis statement, so that everyone involved is clear about what you are testing and the results you are looking for. A hypothesis statement usually has a structure like this: "[Doing something] to [the problematic area] will [have this impact on your chosen KPI]" For example: "Reducing the number of steps in the checkout process from five to three will increase the number of completed purchases." Once you have clearly defined all three of the variables in your hypothesis, you can get started on actually running your tests.

There are a couple of different kinds of test you might want to run, so you will need to be sure to pick the one that is right for your situation. A/B testing (also known as "split" or "bucket" testing) is the simplest form of experimentation in digital marketing. It allows you to focus on a specific conversion goal, such as completing a sale, adding an item to a shopping cart, or submitting a lead form, and to try different versions of one element of your webpage to see which version is best at driving your desired conversions. You might want to try varying the wording of your call to action, or changing the color of a "Buy Now" button. Your original version (the "control") as well as the altered pages (or "variants") are shown at random - but in equal proportion - to visitors. The results are tracked in your analytics until you are confident that an obvious winner has emerged. A/B testing has a couple of key benefits.

Firstly, restricting your tests to just one element or page at a time ensures that any changes shown in your results can almost certainly be attributed to your test. Plus, because A/B tests involve only one variable at a time, they are much easier to set up and evaluate than the more complex multivariate tests. In multivariate testing, many variables on the page are tested simultaneously, with the goal of determining which combination works best. You might try working with several versions of the headline, calls to action, or button designs to see how visitors respond. This technique can be used to optimize landing pages by designing some very different options and gradually putting together and refining the most successful elements.

Because multivariate testing involves multiple combinations of variants, it is more complex to set up, and requires much higher traffic volumes before you can be sure you have found a clear winner.

How do you know when your test is over? If you stop the test too soon, you might not have had enough visitors see each version of your site for the results to be statistically significant. You should only stop the test when you are confident that the results show actual trends which are likely to be repeated - rather than just happening by chance.

If you are using Google Analytics, you can easily set up A/B and multivariate tests using Google Optimize, which is integrated with analytics. Once you have defined what you are testing and provided the control and variants pages, Google will take care of serving the different page versions, and reporting the outcomes. It will also let you know the statistical significance of the results, and it will stop the test automatically as soon as it detects a winner. It might be that over time you need to revisit and revamp the same element of your site several times as your campaigns and audience behaviors change, so do not assume that once you have crossed something off your list, you will never need to look at it again.

Do not forget that testing and learning is a continuous process, so once you have completed one test you should be going back to your data and business priorities and deciding what to improve next – and by doing that, over time you should see your site's performance getting better and better.

PART II
BIG DATA

BIG DATA

THE ORIGINS OF BIG DATA

L et us start with some history. And I mean real history. Long ago, the ancient Romans gathered information from across their far-flung empire to gain insights and make predictions about population. Using this, they could better identify who could be conscripted to join the army and, obviously important to governments then and now: keep an eye on taxes.

The Roman 'census' comes from the Latin for 'assess,' and relied on collecting this information, or "data," which is the Roman plural for bits of it. So, you see, this approach to data was around long before there were computers... In the early 1800s, French mathematician Pierre-Simon LaPlace foreshadowed the insights of data science when he postulated that if a consciousness could know the position of every atom in the universe, nothing would be uncertain and "the future, just like the past, would be present before its eyes."

Data science, as a technology applied to real-world solutions, got serious by the middle of that same century. A famous example of its use was John Snow who, in 1854, collected data on reports of cholera infection and correlated it with the location of water pumps across London. By doing this, he proved that one site — the Broad Street pump — was the source of the outbreak. Perhaps one of the first real-world actions taken based on big data was when the authorities literally took the handle off of the pump, and thereby stalled the spread of the disease.

A little later on, in the 1880s, American astronomer Simon Newcomb noticed a curious pattern in books containing logarithm tables, which were used to help with certain calculations. He found that pages that started with the digit '1' were far more worn than other pages, in other words – people looked at these pages more often.

This principle was revisited in 1938 by physicist Frank Benford, who found that it was much more general than Newcomb had realized, and for any list of numbers taken from an arbitrary set of data, more of those numbers will start with '1' than any other digit.

Because of the success of his 'pattern recognition,' a crucial component of big data projects, 'Benford's Law' has since been used in such diverse applications as fraud detection in accounting and elections, and even understanding prices and genomic data.

For now, it is important to recognize that today's uses of big data are a direct extension of established thinking and practices - although there are some notable differences. The biggest difference, naturally, is the availability of computers, which allow for vastly larger amounts of data to be processed; the more data you have, generally speaking, the better and more reliable your insights can be.

In 1965, Gordon Moore, who was one of the founders of Intel, a giant computer chip maker, plotted the number of transistors that fit on a chip back to 1959, and saw that each year the capacity had doubled. He predicted that the number of transistors on a computer chip would continue to double, first every year into the future and then, a bit later, he revised it to predict it doubling every two years. This prediction - a sort of big data insight itself - known as Moore's Law, has come true.

Just to confirm how far we have traveled, the real-time guidance computer in the Apollo 11 capsule that went to the Moon and back had 64 Kilobytes of memory, and operated at little over 4/100ths of a MegaHertz. To put that in perspective, your smartphone is a million times more powerful than all of NASA's computing was in 1969.

The ability to process more data more often generally translates into better and deeper insights and capabilities. As the power of computers to do calculations has gone up, the cost of doing them has gone down, making it available to more people, more often.

Another big difference since the days of collecting data with pens and paper is, well, we do not have to do it anymore. Our devices do it. Nobody knows the exact number, but estimates of devices connected to the Internet of Things — which means they possess the capacity to sense and process data — range from 6 to 17 billion, which is a huge number…and it promises to keep growing, with predictions that it could hit over 100 billion by 2030(!) Smartphones, home assistants, connected TVs, connected appliances like refrigerators and even toasters…each of these devices not only collects and shares data, but uses it to enable us to do things.

What is changed the most is where we spend a good portion of our lives today. While the experiences of living in the 19th century were defined solely by the limitations of physical space and time, today we can take digital journeys… to stores, to information, or simply to talk with one another. Because our use of the Internet requires digital tools, it generates digital content — data — so our very experiences of living are translated into information.

Using mobile technology means this happens even more frequently, because we use digital tools to accomplish even more tasks.

In 2017, it was estimated that Americans spend almost 11 hours a day staring at a screen of some sort; that is almost half their lives, and certainly a majority of their waking hours. It is safe to assume that much of that time is spent interacting with their devices. And every time we do so… we generate data.

This is the basis for a concept in marketing called the "single customer view," sometimes referred to as the "360-degree view of the customer." This is the holistic picture of who you are and what you like to do and, thus, what you might like to buy, which is derived from data collected via multiple sources and visits online, which is then analyzed for patterns.

Understanding history and preferences, just like Snow and Benford showed centuries ago, helps create a more accurate understanding of patterns, and ultimately, the future.

USES OF BIG DATA

Taken together — computer processing capabilities, the Internet of Things and mobile revolutions, and the time we spend doing things on our digital devices — is how we get to the "big" in "big data." Big amounts of it. Big processing speeds. Big insights and applications.

The most common uses for big data in business continue to be related to marketing and other human-centric behaviors, but only because transactional, social media, and clickstream data are some of the most common and available... because We are all using the Internet so much to do things. But the growth in machine data — the bits of information produced by machines themselves, whether driving down the street or assembling something on a factory production line — is inescapable. Already, some industrial systems can monitor their own performance and send operators signals if something is starting to fail, or if some other problem has emerged. Data from past performance can be used to predict those instances, and allow maintenance to occur before systems are impacted.

The challenge for businesses is to understand such uses, and it means using that understanding to craft business cases, and subsequent approaches for big data. It also means that we should consider what the future of big data may bring... While the marketing uses for big data may be the most common or obvious today, tomorrow's uses for big data can be summed up in two words: Artificial Intelligence, or "AI." AI rivals big data as a popular buzzword, but what is it exactly? The short answer is that there is no standard definition, though the most accurate ones are based on our definition of intelligence in the human sense. Our brains are "intelligent," or so we hope, because we can perceive things in an endless array of diverse situations, from recognizing a stop sign on a sunny day or at night, to intuitively grasping the difference between doing something that is "right" versus something that's "wrong." We tend to equate intelligence with the ability to understand and make distinctions, rather than just being "smart" with command of lots of facts.

Data scientists have a term for this ability — they call it "agency" — and they see it, like we non-data scientists do, as something more than being simply book smart. Intelligence does not arise from possessing information alone, but instead: learning and integrating it into experiences, different ones, over and over again.

Theoretically, we get smarter with every new bit of information we acquire in our lives (or at least… we could!). It is the same for artificial intelligence, too. Another term you might hear in this context is 'machine learning,' which refers to building a system that learns for itself how to complete a specific goal by iterating through possible solutions to a problem and then adjusting its method according to results. This is a type of AI in itself - whereby the system is actively 'learning' rather than being pre-programmed with responses; conducting a process, changing its approach, and repeating in a similar way that a human might. Just like how our brains rely on lots of data, to learn and acquire intelligence, so do computers, but with three differences from our organic approach.

First, computers can acquire data from an all but endless universe of sources, whereas We are limited to what we can perceive with our senses. Sure, we can extend our perception using information we find on the world wide web (or even 'technologies' like eyeglasses, which improve our sight), but in some sense we must admit that we have an upper boundary for capability.

Second, computers can do everything faster, and continue to speed things up, as Moore predicted 50 years ago. Think of the last time you tried to think about a handful of subjects at the same time; it probably felt more like daydreaming or confusion instead of focusing on parallel tracks of information. Thirdly, computers can learn faster than we can, in part because they can process information on different situations faster and more consistently, but also because they can develop new ways to learn from it.

It is understandable that, as we move forward with certain technologies, certain fictional depictions of 'smart devices' or AI stick in our minds. But more certain than such fiction, We are clearly looking at a future in which big data enables far more impactful, and interesting things, than, say... teeing-up your favorite shoe brand or vacation destinations next time you visit Facebook.

In early 2017, an experimental car was able to drive without a programmer having given it instructions; it taught itself by "watching" humans do it. Later in the year, a computer taught itself how to beat the highest ranked human player of the board game 'Go.' In both cases, nobody could say exactly how the computers did it. The process of learning from examples is called "experience replay," and the outcomes are surprising, if not somewhat unsettling... AI will radically transform how we live and work. Imagine an intelligent device that, say, operates all of the systems in your house to maximize energy efficiency, or your car avoiding accidents while finding the best routes to work? What about a smart search of your physical health signs that uses real-time data to map the likelihood of an illness, or an incident of a once unpredictable event, like a heart attack? Imagine a business that can rely on an automated factory to manage its own production line, or a supply chain the tells itself when and where parts are needed... and then gets them to the factory on its own? Of course, that is not the future We are describing... but the present, and the availability of big data combined with computing power makes this possible already. It is believed that two-thirds of consumers are already using technologies that are empowered or assisted by AI.

What will come in the future is more intelligence...more agency...that enables machines to make and implement decisions, based in large part on what they have learned. Smart devices will continue to get smarter. Ultimately, 'big data' in the broadest sense has been with us for thousands of years, and the basic premise of using it was known long before anyone had heard of Siri or said "OK, Google..." Its applications are reality now, as nearly half of the companies in the Fortune 1000 report not just that they are using it, but that they have achieved measurable results doing so. It is worth noting, however, that a majority of them also report that they've yet to successfully begin transforming their businesses into data-driven cultures.

The challenge seems to be as old as the opportunity that big data represents: How can you conceive, organize, operationalize, analyze, and then apply the insights that should come from data about your customers, partners, and from the world at large?

PRIVACY, SECURITY, AND THE FUTURE

By now, you should have a clear picture of how big data fits into the world around us, but before we start looking at how big data projects work, and how to formulate the business case to get them going in your organization, we need to mention a few overarching points that you must always keep in mind...

In a 'big data' world, we really cannot overstate the importance of privacy. The whole point of using big data is to learn things - about people and processes - that might not only be unapparent to you, but they might not even be known by the people you are studying. All of us have habits and behaviors that We are not consciously aware of, or that we purposefully do not want to address. Data science does not recognize this truth, and there is no sense of morality inherent in how systems are programmed or operate. Whatever the context, your project risks telling people things they might be surprised that you know.

Most business processes come down to the actions of people tasked with implementing them. So, unless they have been automated, and as anybody who has been told to do something differently than they have always done it can confirm: this kind of direction can be... less than motivational, if not sometimes too personal.

So it is vitally important that you found your project on respect for people's privacy, and put in place the necessary measures to inform them of what you are doing, allow them to opt-out if they so choose and, in the case of internal staff, help them learn to do things differently, if required. Life would be so much easier if you could simply show people "a better way" and they embraced it without question, but we know that rarely happens, if ever.

These requirements are not just the 'moral' thing to do and smart in a business context, but increasingly government regulators are demanding it. Do not just try to meet whatever the letter of the law might be, since it is more than likely the law will get more stringent over time. Security is closely related to privacy, and it is the second thing you need to always keep in mind. Your data is a valuable asset, which means you are at risk of it being corrupted or stolen. Keeping big data projects secure is different than the practices utilized by your enterprise IT team. Locations can be more distributed, both on the input side — such as your customers' smartphones — as well as the places you process, analyze, and apply it.

Sharing can happen in real-time, which means data is traversing between locations and therefore subject to damage or theft. Indeed, much of the work will likely happen in 'the cloud,' which endures a constant barrage of attacks from hackers and other malicious types. And, if you are in the industrial space and using your big data conclusions to operate machines, you risk having those commands interrupted or replaced with well... not the right ones.

Hackers have already broken into the computer controls of cars and airplanes. You do not want your project to be added to that list. By the way, this includes preventing any misuse of the data by your team or any vendors or suppliers with whom you are working. In the same sense that the hottest new books often get 'leaked' by printers or bookstores involved in bringing them to market, you need to take steps to minimize the risk that one of your employees or an external resource might have the capability - or even incentive - to violate your trust. Finally, a quick comment on the subject of "big tech" in general.

Despite all of its applications in AI and automating our lives, and the tech giants that now dominate the online landscape... the future of big data is not set in stone. Not only is that future unwritten, so we do not know what it is going to look like exactly, but there are rigorous debates underway regarding its uses from social, moral, and legal perspectives. Legitimate questions are being asked about whether consumers, and citizens, should have more input and control over it. It will be fascinating to see how things play out, but in the meantime, it should encourage you to intensify your efforts to consider any big data project within the context of your overt and implicit relationships with your customers, external stakeholders, and within your business.

CAPTURE, PROCESS, VISUALIZE, ANALYZE, APPLY AND REVERT

If we wanted to map how a factory works, we would probably start with a description of the manufacturing process, but not necessarily focus on descriptions of particular jobs or machines placed along the production line. Instead, we would start with a simple angle: this is what starts at the front end, and here are the basic steps taken to produce so-and so output at the back end. Afterwards, there would be any amount of detailed descriptions of what those steps might be, and the technologies used to accomplish them.

So, let us approach a big data project in the same way. Any big data project involves seven core activities.

Some of these can be accomplished independently of others, in other words, you do not have to do all seven activities every time you want to execute a project, but all seven activities are reflected in, or used by, any project you might take on.

Capture

As you might guess, is the act of collecting information, or data. It is the starting point for any project because data is a raw resource…and we mean raw because data can come in many formats. The important line that helps us define data separates "structured" from "unstructured" data…

Structured data is anything that has been entered into an established form or process for capturing it; think of the fields you have been asked to fill out when ordering something from an online store, or employee records entered into a database intended to track whatever qualities your company wants to remember. It is also data that has been collected automatically, such as repeat visits to a website from a particular shopper, or a smart streetlamp that captures the volume of traffic that passes by.

This data can be easily searched by an algorithm, which is simply a kind of program that solves a problem through a specific set of operations. So, you can, quite literally, tell it where to look and what to compare, whether you are interested in numbers or words. It is the 'relational capacity' of structured data — the ability to make "apples to apples" comparisons — that makes it useful. Chances are that your company possesses lots of this data, especially as it relates to your customers – which is why big data is used so often by marketers.

Unstructured data is, quite simply, everything else. Emails are unstructured data, as are text messages. The information contained in a video or audio recording is unstructured (and, so far, actually impossible for consumers to search). In fact, the entire World Wide Web consists of unstructured data, which is what Google helps overcome by using crawlers and other tools to capture information that can be used to create somewhat similar, and therefore comparable descriptions of what wildly different websites contain. It is difficult for most companies to use unstructured data.

The easiest and most profitable big data solutions will likely rely on structured data, whether you already possess it, or design a project to capture it. The distinctions between structured and unstructured data should not really impact the capture phase of a project, however, in that that you do not really want to preclude information until you have a full view of what is available to you.

So, the capture phase usually involves feeding all sorts of data into something called a "data lake," which is literally what the name implies. The non-technical aspect of the capture phase is having visibility into what you know about something... not conclusions, but what information about a subject is available to you.

Process

Which is where companies define what they want to look at, how they are going to do it, and all the while guided by a clear picture of why. When it comes to processing your data, you do not always need an exact idea of what you think the data will show you, but instead, a reason for why you want to look at X, Y, or Z. Your process could be guided by a declarative intention, such as: "I want to improve production scheduling, so I want to know what times during the day our suppliers make deliveries, and correlate that with the weather." Or you might just have a more general curiosity about impacts on deliveries and therefore include more data variables in your process.

Put simply, people tend to find what they are looking for, so the key to a successful process is to know what data you want to look at more than forcing the outcome you think you want to find. Successful data science relies on posing good questions more than dictating exactly what will be the best or most important sources for answers.

What matters is the "how" of your process, or what you want to compare, or relate. Think of John Snow and his decision to correlate outbreaks of cholera in London with the locations of water pumps; what drove that process was his assumption that there might be a connection, but he could have just as easily looked at incidences of the disease correlated with bakeries, or some other variables. He just happened to be looking to prove or disprove a very specific hypothesis, and it turned out that he was correct. The relative ease of today's computational power allows us to pose broader, and more numerous hypotheses.

Visualize

As all of us can remember at least one instance of being presented with, say, a huge spreadsheet of information and asking ourselves "what exactly am I looking at, or looking for?" A whole host of formats can be used for data visualization, and there are any number of software tools available to render them.

The important parameters of visualization are what data do you want to see, how do you want to express the relationships within and between them, and how much do you want to interact with it (and change the connections or other parameters to yield different insights). The answer to the "what data?" question should be reasonably obvious, since it is mainly determined by what information you chose to study in the process. How you express it can get really interesting and fun, since there are many ways to do it.

Numeric representation is the most obvious, and a few columns of numbers do not have to be mind-numbingly boring, especially if you have wisely used colors, highlighting, and so on. What is good about expressing output in numbers is that the format, often a spreadsheet, is easily shared. Charts are also sharable, and can be far more impactful. If your output is in words, you can use things like word clouds to communicate importance and relationships. Maps are also very commonly used in big data projects, because location can play such an important role in understanding the behaviors of customers, suppliers, and other groups.

You will often see a few, or many of these outputs aggregated into dashboards, which are used by marketers to track aspects of customer behavior or, in growing numbers, various aspects of healthcare big data insights. Beyond these, with a little research and expertise there are some seriously interesting ways to visualize your output, such as using 3D rendering, which is sometimes used to simulate the interaction between multiple data points. The trick here is to ensure that your visualization matches the needs and tastes of the people who need to consume and use the data.

There is no "right" answer other than meeting that requirement, and enabling your users to literally see clearly the correlations that your data process reveals.

Store

We are not going to spend a lot of time on the next destination on our roadmap — which is Store — because how and where your big data results are stored is something that an actual IT person needs to decide, and manage from there. This is not to downplay its importance at all – it is just that the technical qualities of that activity are handled by specialists, and rightly so. Dealing with consumer data means you must keep up-to-date with changes in legislation, as governmental bodies in Europe, the US and elsewhere are currently refining their attitudes towards privacy, security, and transparency.

Keeping data secure is made that much more complex when it is constantly travelling between locations, and the cloud obviously carries a whole host of potential risks. And it is not just for the benefit of all the people whose data you are handling, various "duty to notify laws" require you to inform users and partners of breaches, something that could trigger civil fines and litigation. Failure to notify might be a serious criminal offence. Also, your data and insights are valuable assets that a competitor might want to access, or a hacker might want to kidnap and hold for ransom via encryption... or simply destroy for the sheer sake of it. Normal enterprise IT security protocols need to be revisited in such cases, especially since it is likely a big data project will span multiple touchpoints.

As a client or user of big data, your security protections should be as important to you as the insights your data might yield. This includes developing usage rules for who can access the information, from where, and what rights they possess to change or download the data. And most importantly – always follow digital security best practice to keep risk to a minimum.

Analyze and Apply

And it is where things really get going. Analysis means reaching conclusions, or newer hypotheses, based on the data you have visualized. A common analytic tool is called "segmentation," which simply means putting like evidenced data into the same segment, bucket, or group.

Analysis of your data might tell you that certain customers buy at certain times each day, but only from certain locations. It might reveal that employees whose initial resumes longer tend to stay employed for fewer months than those with shorter ones, or that lights in offices that are turned off fewer than 3 times a day last longer than those that are turned off more often. The number of analytic outcomes is truly infinite; so what you want to do in this step is draw the conclusions that are most overt, supported by the most data points, and create in your mind (and not only on a computer screen) a group of people, or events, which are similar. Not surprisingly, segmentation has proven uses in marketing, where you can collect similar customers into a group or class that is identified by shared attributes, and then create communications tailored for them. But it is just as easily applied to devices or events...any set of variables from which patterns might emerge. Studies of prices, for instance, can be modelled in this way. So can the probability of business outcomes, so imagine analyzing how sales or partnership deals are completed.

Usually, the Analyze stage means identifying strong correlation between variables; your data cannot prove causation, in and of itself, but it can make it 'all but certain,' at least enough so that you can make business decisions based on it. It is worth stressing that your big data analysis will not tell you why things happen, or are connected, but only that they seem to be, perhaps consistently and inescapably. That is why the analysis step is as much about your business strategy processes as anything else; big data will not tell you what to do, but it will show you the potential for doing things.

It is also when you revisit the hypotheses or assumptions that you formulated at the beginning of the project, and ask yourself if the visualized findings prove or disprove them. It is also where you need to keep your mind open to discovering unexpected patterns, or the lack of ones you otherwise assumed existed, and brainstorm what that might mean.

You can tell that We are making the transition back to the 'real world' here, and your work in analyzing your data leads directly into the next step, which is to Apply it. Are there potential opportunities to... say different things to different groups? Sell more, or differently? Change the scheduling in a process? Or provide service in some new, better way? Again, the marketing world gives us some straightforward examples to follow. Marketers tend to 'target' segments of customers, based on the conclusions they reached in the analyze phase of their big data projects, and then act upon that information. They often use something called a data management platform, or 'DMP,' to develop those targets, and then manage how they change communications to, and with them, accordingly. This is just a common example, but you can target just about anything.

However, it is important to note here that some expert reports suggest that 85% of big data projects fail to meet their goals, and most of those failures actually occur in the Apply stage. In other words, companies get the data they wanted, but are not able to put it to use successfully. This obviously raises questions about organizational change and empowerment, which are probably outside the scope of anything a big data project could hope to impact.

Revert is the final step, which is when you take what you have learned, feed it back into the process, and do it again…only better. Constant iteration is a hallmark not just of good big data practices, but of any agile or innovative company. However, you go about it, every pattern you perceive in your data may well suggest a new opportunity to look for correlation.

SCOPE AND RISKS

If our roadmap for big data projects has seven steps to it, then there are also four qualities that define the map's scope. These are the things that determine your requirements for resources, expertise, time, and your stomach for risk. They all start with the letter "V," and they are all interrelated. Volume is the first property, as there are data lakes, and then there are data lakes that look like deep oceans.

Your ability to acquire data is only as good as your ability to store it, and your ability to store it directly impacts what you can do with it. Put simply, more volume involved in your big data project means more work and cost. Velocity is the speed at which the data is acquired to your network, or shared within it.

Crunching vast amounts of information can slow down a network, and delay delivery of your results, and most enterprise IT systems are not configured to handle it. Just think of how slow your desktop can get if it is trying to do too many things at once. This property becomes especially relevant when you consider the data that can come into your network automatically, from devices connected to the Internet of Things.

The third property is Variety, which speaks to the diversity of data in your data lake. Data lakes can contain both structured and unstructured data and that data can come in many different formats. If your data lake is diverse as well as deep, your big data project will need to account for it.

Finally, the fourth property is Veracity: how reliably accurate is your data (whether due to presentation format or the fundamental substance of it)? A bad set of numbers will yield the wrong conclusions, obviously. When combined, a big data project roadmap and its scope are the tools with which you work to solve business problems.

Understanding those building blocks will make you better able to design your project, as a businessperson and not a data science expert, as well as perform as an informed participant in conversations about its development and delivery.

Taking on big data projects requires an understanding of the distinction between correlation and causation. Let us say I notice that most days I am in a bad mood, it is also poor weather outside. Do my moods cause the bad weather? Of course not. Does the weather cause my bad moods? Well, that is at least more possible, but the real answer is that I have no idea. I have correlated the two data points — there may be something there — but I have not proven causation. The biggest risk in using big data is to confuse correlation with causation.

Also, there is no supercomputer that can give the right answer to any question asked of it; even IBM's Watson only knows what it knows. Further, no amount of modelling past behavior will guarantee that the future will occur in an identical or specific way. All we can aspire to do is to make the indications of correlation more suggestively certain. The best way to accomplish this, and to minimize any potential risk of failure is to limit the scope of the project. By definition, smaller questions are going to be more reliable than bigger ones, since they require fewer leaps of faith. If we consider the marketing use of big data, the question of "why customers buy" is actually a series of questions that are dependent on one another in a fairly linear manner. You might want to approach your big data projects as a similar set of smaller ones, and build your journey toward your "bigger" conclusion.

This also lets you test each conclusion in the real world, which will contribute to improving the reliability of your journey as it progresses. Each big data project will of course differ, but if you are armed with an understanding of the general 'roadmap,' what's involved in scoping projects and keep your expectations in check about what you are likely or able to achieve, then you are sure to be on the right track.

GLOSSARY

A/B Testing (also known as "split" or "bucket" testing) In A/B testing an element of a website, for example the color of the "Buy Now" button, is varied; and both the original and altered pages are shown at random, in equal proportion, to visitors.

Acquisition KPIs are metrics that measure how well you are attracting visitors to your site, for example share of search, or click-through rate.

Agency is the term data scientists use to describe the ability to learn, understand and make decisions.

Analytics Vendor Data Analytics is a data source used by competitive intelligence tools, in which vendors such as Google Analytics collect anonymized information including sites visited, keywords searched, and sometimes browsers and devices used.

Artificial Intelligence There is no standard definition for Artificial Intelligence, though the most accurate ones are based on our own understanding of intelligence in the human sense - that being, the ability to learn, understand and make decisions, or as data scientists call it, "agency." Experience Replay The process of learning from examples.

Audience Report shows you information about the characteristics of your visitors, including whether they are new to your site and geographic location.

Audience Segmentation in the process of breaking your audience down into target subgroups according to shared characteristics, such as location, age, or consumer behavior. This can be done through the segments function of your analytics tool.

Behavior KPIs are metrics that relate to the actions that visitors take on your site outside of purchases and conversions, for example visitor loyalty, or bounce rate.

Behavior Report shows you information about what visitors do once they are actually on your site, with a focus on activities other than purchases (which is covered in the Conversions section).

Bounce Rate measures the amount of people who exit a site without making a second click.

Competitive Intelligence refers to information on the overall environment a business is operating in, including information surrounding the progress of competitors.

Control in A/B and multivariate testing, "control" refers to the original version of the website area or page that you are testing.

Conversion A conversion is the main action you want a user to take as a result of visiting your site, for example making a purchase or signing up to a newsletter. Your conversion rate is the percentage of visitors to your site who end up taking this desired action.

Conversion KPIs are metrics that relate to business outcomes, for example evaluating how compelling your calls to action are, or the usability of your site. These include conversion rate, or total goal value.

Conversions Report shows you information about how well your site is driving transactions, leads, and any other interactions that you have defined.

Dashboard Dashboards are a way of presenting your analytics findings; usually featuring one page (or screen) of information which shows what is happening in critical areas, how well your most important KPIs are doing, and how your results are trending over time.

Data Lake A storage repository for the raw data gleaned from the capture process of a big data project.

Dimensions are the attributes of your data that you are measuring, for example the different countries your visitors are coming from. Dimensions form the rows of your analytics reports.

Direct Traffic refers to visitors who come to a site without clicking on a link or going through a search engine, implying that they already know the URL or had the site bookmarked.

DMP (Data Management Platform) A piece of software that warehouses and analyses audience data for media companies. DMPs are often used to manage Deal IDs and create audience segments for targeting purposes. Data from DMPs is often fed into Demand Side Platforms to inform buying decisions.

eCommerce Report shows you information about product performance, shopping behavior, and checkout behavior. This type of report is only applicable to sites that sell products directly.

Events are the individual actions taken by a user during a session, for example clicking links, watching videos, and downloading files.

Event Action ('Event action') is a field value in event tracking which refers to the specific action taken by the user. If your category is video, your actions may include play, pause, or view.

Event Category ('Event category') is a field value in event tracking which groups certain types of elements together, for example video, PDF, or button.

Event Label ('Event label') is a field value in event tracking which allows you to name individual items within the same category. If your category is video, your labels may be 'intro video' or 'June promotional video.'

Filters are divisions that can be permanently applied to data, used to ensure that analytics reports never contain information deemed distracting or irrelevant.

Hypothesis Statement A hypothesis statement is a statement of the theory behind a test, which will be proved or disproved when you come to evaluate your results. A hypothesis statement usually conforms to the following structure: "[Doing something] to [the problematic area] will [have this impact on your chosen KPI]."

Internet of Things (IoT) A development of the existing computer-based internet paradigm in which thousands of previously inert objects are internet-enabled, with the ability to sense and process data. Machine Data Bits of information produced by machines themselves.

Internet Service Provider Data is a data source used by competitive intelligence tools, in which Internet Service Providers (ISPs) collect anonymized information including sites visited, keywords searched, and sometimes browsers and devices used.

Metrics are the numerical values – usually percentages or ratios - assigned to the data you are measuring. Metrics form the columns of your analytics reports.

Multi-Channel Attribution A multi-channel attribution report displays information regarding all the channels visitors are using leading up to conversions, and assigns different values to each one according to the impact they are having. This is found in the Conversions section of your analytics tool

Multivariate Testing In multivariate testing, many variables on a page are tested simultaneously, with the goal of determining which combination works best. For example, you might try working with several versions of the headline, calls to action, or button designs to see how visitors respond.

Panel Data is a data source used by competitive intelligence tools, in which a group of participants agree to install monitoring software which then tracks their browsing behavior.

Purchase Funnel Analysis is an analysis of the specific steps customers are taking in order to convert on your site, and where they are dropping off. This is found in the Conversions section of your analytics tool.

Real-Time Report shows you live information about visitors who are currently on your site, including which pages they are on and demographic information.

Referrals are visitors who arrive at your site by clicking on a link from another website. This is displayed through the referral path in an analytics report.

Machine Learning refers to building a system that learns for itself how to complete a specific goal by iterating through possible solutions to a problem and then adjusting its method according to the results.

Segmentation A common analytics tool in which you put like-evidenced data into the same segment or group. Structured data Information that has been entered, potentially automatically, into an established form or process for capturing, which can be easily searched by an algorithm. For example, this could be a purchase form, employee records, repeat visits to a website by a particular user, spreadsheets, or even the volume of traffic that passes by a smart streetlamp.

Self-Reported Data is a data source used by competitive intelligence tools, in which website owners agree to report their own data to competitive intelligence companies.

Server Log is a tool used to collect analytics data. When a user arrives at a site, a request is sent to the web server where your site is hosted. The web server makes a log entry which contains visitor information, which can then be accessed by analytics tools.

Session is the continuous period of that time a user spends on a site. The session ends when the visitor has not done anything for a specified amount of time, usually 30 minutes.

Tracking Code/Tag is a tool used to collect analytics data. Tags are placed into areas of your website you wish to track. When a user takes the relevant action, the script executes and collects data, for example where the visitor is located and what browser they are using.

Unique Visitors (or users) are the number of different individuals who visit your site.

Unstructured data is information that is not presented in an established form or process, which is harder to search for and use in big data projects compared to structured data. Examples of unstructured data include emails, text messages, written reviews, as well as video and audio recordings.

Variant In A/B and multivariate testing, "variant" refers to the altered version of the website area of page that you are testing. Web Crawler Data Web crawler data is a data source used by competitive intelligence tools, in which competitive analysis companies use their own set of crawlers to scan publicly available websites.

ABOUT JULIAN DELPHIKI

Julian Delphiki is a pseudonym, created to safeguard the integrity of his personal identity and ensure that the focus remains on transformative ideas rather than the individual. This philosophical stance permeates every aspect of his work, from his senior role in a renowned multinational company to his more private collaborations such as one-on-one executive coaching sessions.

For more than two decades, Julian has successfully navigated demanding environments in both well-established corporations and cutting-edge startups in pioneering eCommerce sectors such as fashion. This extensive journey has shaped him into a multifaceted professional whose expertise is not merely theoretical but firmly rooted in practical application. As a seasoned professional, he has honed his skills across diverse functions—ranging from managing complex projects to leadership and activation—consistently delivering results that reflect his unwavering commitment to the success of every initiative.

His strategic vision and adaptability have made him a pragmatic visionary, capable of understanding the needs of the market, businesses, and audiences alike. Beyond his corporate career, Julian is the founder and principal consultant of his own firm, where he channels this experience to help organizations of all kinds optimize their operations and achieve sustainable growth. His work in this space often spans digital marketing, online business, and, more broadly, business management and productivity.

Yet Julian's influence extends far beyond the executive committee. He is also a prominent figure in the realms of personal development and philosophical exploration. As a lecturer in various universities and business schools, he is also a dedicated coach, devoting his energy and passion to fostering personal growth. His coaching philosophy embraces a holistic approach, carefully intertwining personal development with philosophical introspection. This dual perspective enables him to delve deeply into the nuances of critical issues in the social sciences. With a genuine passion for empowering individuals to reach their fullest potential, Julian engages in inspirational and transformative conversations while offering practical tools to catalyze positive change in people's lives.

The fusion of Julian Delphiki's professional and personal spheres creates a truly unique mosaic of skills, knowledge, and a profound commitment to enhancing individuals, organizations, and society as a whole. His ability to bridge the strategic demands of the professional world with the deep self-knowledge required for personal growth provides an extraordinary lens through which to understand human behavior and psychology, the direction of businesses, and the evolution of society.

This interdisciplinary foundation makes him a compelling voice, capable of publishing thought-provoking books on a wide range of topics—united by his core mission of fostering growth and understanding in a complex world.

OTHER BOOKS BY THE AUTHOR

La abolición del trabajo. BLACK, BOB and DELPHIKI, JULIAN. 2024.

Maestros del hábito. DELPHIKI, JULIAN. 2023.

Modern philosophers. DELPHIKI, JULIAN. 2022

A modern hero. DELPHIKI, JULIAN. 2022.

Folkhorror volume I. DELPHIKI, JULIAN. 2022.

Ad tech and programmatic. DELPHIKI, JULIAN. 2020.

eCommerce 360. English edition. DELPHIKI, JULIAN. 2020.

eCommerce 360. Spanish edition. DELPHIKI, JULIAN. 2020.

Content marketing and online video marketing. DELPHIKI, JULIAN. 2020.

Digital transformation. DELPHIKI, JULIAN. 2020.

Optimizing SEO and paid search fundamentals. DELPHIKI, JULIAN. 2020.

Social media business. DELPHIKI, JULIAN. 2020.

Tales of horror and history. DELPHIKI, JULIAN. 2020.

Web Analytics and Big Data. English edition. DELPHIKI, JULIAN. 2020.

Analítica web y móvil. Spanish edition. DELPHIKI, JULIAN. 2019.

www.ingramcontent.com/pod-product-compliance
Lightning Source LLC
Chambersburg PA
CBHW051538240526
45465CB00027B/617